THE
PURPOSE
PUZZLE

THE PURPOSE PUZZLE

JULIE K.

XULON PRESS

Xulon Press
2301 Lucien Way #415
Maitland, FL 32751
407.339.4217
www.xulonpress.com

Paperback ISBN-13: 978-1-66284-143-9
Ebook ISBN-13: 978-1-66284-144-6

DEDICATION

I WOULD LIKE to dedicate my book to my husband and to my children, who I love very, very much! To my family and friends who have been by my side throughout this journey, and to so many of you that read this and encouraged me to share my story, I appreciate you believing in me! And, finally, I would like to dedicate this to anyone and everyone who has been touched by the blessing of adoption.

TABLE OF CONTENTS

Introduction

I HAVE FOUND my purpose in the puzzle that is my life. It is truly a story of unconditional love that Papa God has shown me throughout my life. I hope you will read my stories and hear my voice in these pages. I hope you will laugh with me (or at me), cry along with me, be touched in your own life with one of my "life lessons", but most importantly know that there is nothing that will ever cause God to turn his back on us. Even when we don't feel it, He is working in our lives. And, now, I challenge you to find YOUR PURPOSE!

PURPOSE. What a simple word, but can mean so many different things. If you look in the dictionary, there are several meanings of the word purpose. It can mean a person's sense of resolve or determination, like "his purpose for the meeting was to mend a relationship." It can mean a particular requirement or consideration, like "file this for tax purposes." Over the past two years, this word has been "my word" and has a NEW and totally DIFFERENT meaning. And, I'd like to share what the word PURPOSE means to me.

A dear friend, Terry, who has also been a mentor, encourager and spiritual powerhouse in my life challenged me by asking "What is your purpose? Do you know what it is?" I immediately thought, *"I got this. This is an easy one."* I answered her by saying, "My purpose is to be a mom." She looked at me like I was crazy and said, "Naw. That has nothing to do with YOU, Julie." I tried to justify my answer in my own brain by thinking that I loved my kids and basically felt like that was the "job" I did and honestly, I poured my heart and soul into my family. I felt like MY FAMILY was MY PURPOSE. Wrong!

So then I thought my purpose must be my actual job. I work for my father's company and basically have all of my life. His machine shop began in our basement where I grew up, and I remember learning to engrave when I was just 9 years old. I also built my very own set of braces and would pretend that I was an orthodontist. I used to love to be "working" in the basement with my dad and to this day, I love the smell of metal. Over the years that I have worked at the company, I have done a little bit of everything on the administrative side. I am currently working side by side with my brother in our motorcycle parts department. Needless to say, the business that started in our basement has grown!

I also have another job, WHICH I LOVE, where I work for Chikondi Health Foundation. It "fills my cup" and makes me see the "bigger picture." CHF runs a hospital in Malawi, Africa (yes, all the way in Africa) and I truly love the work and the BEAUTIFUL people in Malawi. So...surely the job that I have had all of my life (my father's machine shop) and the job that I LOVE (CHF) must mean that MY WORK is my purpose. Wrong Again! And this began my search for MY PURPOSE. (More about Chikondi later in my story!)

I was given a book by my friend to help me on this journey. The book is called "The On Purpose Person" by Kevin W. McCarthy. (I highly recommend this book and I have bought several copies and given them away encourage people to find their purpose.) The book is about a man who goes on his own journey to discover his purpose. He meets with several people who already know their purpose. One of the people that knew their purpose was a young girl. Very young, only a senior in high school. I was amazed and I will admit a bit jealous that she already knew her purpose and I was getting close to 50 years old and had no idea what my purpose was or how to discover it. I finished the book and thought long and hard and came up with MY PURPOSE, which I will share later. (I mean, I do want you to read all I have to say and not stop here!)

So here it goes, MY STORY and MY PURPOSE.

My name is Juliann, but everyone calls me Julie. I got the nickname "Julie K" when I was in school and It has stayed with me all of these years. I am married to my husband Darrell. We have been married for 27 years. I am the proud mother to my children, who I adore! I am a Christian and I love Jesus. I recently turned 51 (cannot believe it) and I have lived such a blessed life.

I was adopted when I was a baby and adoption plays a HUGE role in my life. I am an advocate for adoption and I wish that I could talk everyone into adopting, because it is a true gift. Adopted folks will understand 100%! (More about adoption in my story!)

Like I said earlier, I work for my father's company and I have the pleasure of working with my husband, my brother, niece and my brother-in-law. It is a true family business and our employees feel like family to me! Many of them have seen me grow up and are still part of my life. I also work for Chikondi Health Foundation and as I stated earlier, I absolutely love that job. I visited Malawi for the first time in 2013 and again in 2019. I am planning on going back as much as I can because once you go, you fall in love with the beautiful people and you leave a piece of your heart there. It is still hard for me to realize that a hospital, all the way across the world, is being ran in my hometown and that I am a part of that!

Before I got hired for my job at Chikondi Health Foundation, Wes, our pastor, preached a message about Moses. Moses was born at a time when the Pharaoh attempted to kill all of the newborn males. Moses' mother placed him in a basket and he was placed in the Nile River. His sister Miriam watched after him while he was on the river to make sure he was safe. He was found by Pharaoh's daughter and she raised him as her own. (See, I told you you would see more about adoption!).

The thing that really struck me in our pastor's message was that Moses felt he was not "qualified" to do God's work and to fulfill his purpose. BUT..."God does not call the qualified, He qualifies the called!" God gave Moses everything he needed to lead His people. I felt like our pastor was speaking directly to me. I took the job, even though I was unsure of myself and my abilities. But, I knew God would EQUIP me everything I needed to do this job.

I feel certain He will "equip" me with everything I need to share my story now. And, here is a funny thing, I looked up the meaning of the word EQUIP. It means "to supply with the necessary items for a particular PURPOSE."

I hope that my story will encourage you to search for your purpose. When you know, YOU KNOW! And what a blessing it is!

"To everything there is a season, A time for every purpose under heaven..." Ecclesiastes 3:1

My Beautiful Family

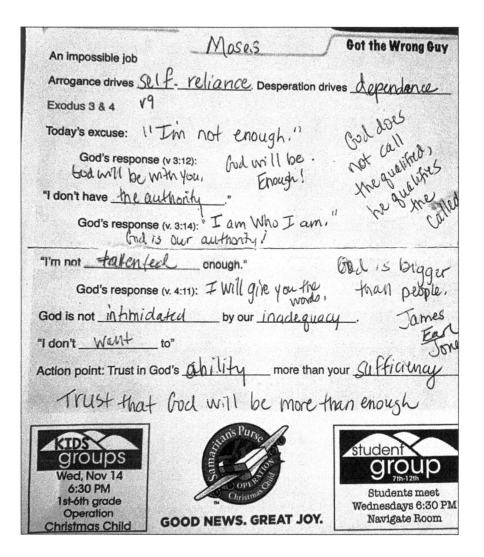

The actual sermon notes taught by my Pastor Wes.
"God does not call the qualified, He qualifies the called!"

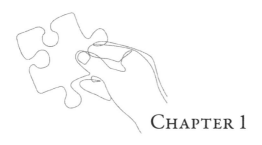

CHAPTER 1

AN IMMIGRANT, A
HEARTBREAK AND ONE

IN MARCH 1888, a young man named Thomas, born in Great Britain, had dreams of a better life and wanted to come over to the United States. Thomas was an immigrant and became a United States Citizen in Jefferson County, Alabama in March,1888.(I actually have his US Citizen paper!) He met a beautiful woman named Elsie Rutledge and they were married. They had two beautiful children, Will and Tom Jr. When the children were very young, they lost their mother to an illness. It was heartbreaking to them all. Their father did not think that he could work and take care of all of the children so he remarried a woman named Isabelle. Isabelle had lost her husband and children of her own that she was trying to raise as a single mother. Her children were Will, Bessie and George Rutledge. These two basically had an agreement to become a family to help each other. Thomas and Isabelle married and had four more children Myrtle, Esther, Ruth and Phillip Earl. They had a total of nine children.

Time passed and two families became one. I will say it again. These two families became one. I truly believe that this was the "seed" that was planted for my life way back then. And although, theirs was no "official adoption" of the children by the parents, this was an act of the self-less love of adoption.

All of the children married and started their own families. Phillip Earl, who was the oldest son of this immigrant couple, is my grandfather. He was born in 1905, grew up in Pratt City, Alabama and worked for Cowan Supply. He met my grandmother, Pauline Gibson, who was a nurse, and they fell in love. I knew that they were crazy about each other because I have some of the love letters they had written each other. I treasure those and would not trade them for anything. My grandfather, Phillip and my grandmother Pauline married and had my mother, Polly Ann in 1939.

My Paw Paw was probably my favorite person on earth when I was little. He was the definition of JOY! The minute his feet hit the floor in the morning, he was happy.So happy, he whistled. And he would usually whistle all day long. He was always loving. He had a place on the lake and it was my second home. He would let me come visit for weeks at a time, and I would pack up all of my toys in my room to go to the lake with me. Like I said, he was pure JOY! He never went to church that I remember. I never really asked him why, but somehow, deep down inside, I thought that he felt that he wasn't good enough for church. (More later on that.) He was so precious to me and the day he passed away, my heart was broken. I remember the conversation that he had with my parents a few days before he died. He was 90 years old and was telling my parents that he thought it may be time to give up driving. That would mean giving up his independence. He never had to give it up, because the Lord took him before he had to. What a gift of perfect timing!

I had said before that my grandmother was a nurse. She was also the best "bacon-cooker"in the south. When I would go and stay at the lake with them, she would make me a pound of bacon and I would eat it up! And somehow, she made it perfect every single time! She loved having us around. She was very sweet and I loved watching her put combs in her hair and to put on her lipstick for church. I also remember that when she would take us to her church, a tiny, country church and we would go and sit on the second row every Sunday. I vividly remember hearing her sing many church hymns. I would put my head on her shoulder and just "absorb" her voice.

Packed and Ready to go with my Grandparents

I just recently found out that she actually helped start a church in Jasper, Alabama. I had no idea about this and I am so proud to know this about her. I wonder how many people's lives were touched by attending the church that she helped to start. The church is still there today. So thankful that I know that information!

She lived four years after my Paw Paw died. The Lord took her peacefully in her sleep. She had been in a nursing home and the nurse called me to tell me that my grandmother was breathing slower than normal and that I should come. I flew down the interstate to get there, but, she had passed already. Like I said, she passed in her sleep, peacefully. I got there before my mother and had to tell her the news. I was so thankful I got there before my mom, because she fell apart. I was able to make decisions that my mom might have not been able to at that time. Once again, God's timing.

Now that I have mentioned my mother Polly, I will go ahead with her story.

"...and the two shall become one. So they are no longer two, but one." Mark 10:8 GNB

My Grandparents at My Wedding

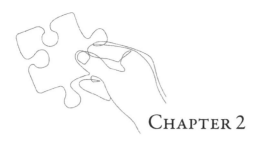

CHAPTER 2

POLLY ANN, MY GUILT AND MY PEACE

My MOTHER WAS born in Montgomery, Alabama on July 10, 1939. She grew up in Montgomery and graduated from Lee High School in 1957, where she met my father, Ken. They married in 1964 and stayed married until she passed away in 2011. She was the most creative woman! She and her best friend Patsy would stay up until all hours sewing what they called "Quiet Books". These books were made to help keep children quiet during church. They were made of fabric and had all sorts of quiet activities in them. My favorite in my book was a page that had a little pink felt hand on it. Sewn onto the hand was a real, beautiful ring. You were supposed to slip your finger right into the ring. There was a poem that said, "Slip on this ring, and you'll feel like a king." If I was to make an adult version of a quiet book, that page would be a little different. It would say, "If you want REAL BLING, Trust JESUS IS KING!" Ha!

She was also the glue that held our family together. Family was important to her and most of our family vacations growing up were spent with cousins or Aunts. One summer, we went and stayed at our cousins' farm in Jasper. They had a huge farm with cattle, a few chickens and some loud guineas. They were so interesting to me and once again LOUD. They rousted in tall trees and would holler anytime something seemed wrong to them. I loved going out and getting fresh eggs every morning and my cousin Elaine would cook for us all. She would cook eggs, sausage, gravy and the best home-made biscuits you ever put in your mouth! She made us all feel so loved by making every single meal seem like a feast. Her husband, Jack, was so funny and spent a lot of time with us on the farm. I got some of my driving skills from him, because I learned early that if I asked sweetly and asked enough times, that he would let me drive all over the farm. All of my younger cousins would make a huge deal about us being there and that made us feel so good. It was like summer camp for me and my brother, but even better! I am bringing up these memories because family is so important. So is opening up your home. I fail miserably at this. My house is always a mess and I get too busy sometimes to keep up with my family. But family is important and so is opening up your home. I need to make others feel like my cousins made me feel.

I feel like I need to mention that my mom lived with an alcoholic father. Yes, my grandfather, who I adored, was an alcoholic. I never knew it until I was an adult. In my eyes, he was wonderful and loving, and my mother, to her credit, never let me think any differently. I will never know her struggle with having an alcoholic father, and I am sure it was very difficult on her and my grandmother. I do believe that everyone who struggles with any addiction, has a reason for that addiction. No one WANTS to be an addict. Maybe it was the loss of his mother at a young age that caused his addiction. But maybe him being an alcoholic was that "seed" that was planted in me, because I do not judge anyone who struggles in that way. Lord bless those that do.

Back to my Mom. My mother also NEVER missed anything I ever did. Whether it was cheering, softball or singing in our chorus at school, she was there. She drove carloads of kids to field trips or games and made sure she was room mother every year at school.

My mom could also wrap presents like no one else I knew. They were almost too pretty to unwrap! She spent as much time on wrapping gifts as she did picking them out.I think it was another way she made people feel special. She would spend a lot of time delivering those gifts. She would jump in her car and drive all over town (sometimes out of town too!) One story that I love to tell about her is about her delivering a gift to our friend Craig, who was struggling with cancer. I knew that he was very sick and his immunity was very low. He also was undergoing treatments and pretty much had a "no visitor" rule for him. My mom insisted on buying Craig pajamas. I kept putting her off telling her that he probably had plenty of pajamas and kept telling her that he was not supposed to have visitors. Well, my mom would not have it. My mom called my friend Kelly (who you will read more about) and had her come pick her up, take her shopping and then deliver the pajamas to Craig. Craig passed away a few weeks later. We were all heart-broken. I remember running into Craig's wife shortly after my mom passed away. We were both standing in front of Target crying talking about how sad we were and how much we missed both my mom and Craig. She quickly told me a verse that had given her some peace. It is Psalm 90:4, "For you, a thousand years is only a short time. They pass as quickly as a day for you..." She explained that here on earth, time goes by a lot slower than for our loved ones in heaven. That gave me such peace knowing that to my mom, it would be a short time before she saw us again. So thankful that God put us both in the same place at the same time so she could share that verse with me. (I have shared it with lots of people who are grieving.) We said our goodbyes, I hugged her and right before I walked away, she casually mentioned this to me. "Oh, by the way, Craig absolutely loved the pajamas that your mom brought him. They were the only things that felt good on his skin in his last days." Thank you again Lord for putting me there to hear those words. My lesson here...Go out of your way to bring joy and comfort to others. (Ouch.)

I said earlier that I was adopted. My mother had to have a hysterectomy when she was 24 and was not able to have children. They chose to adopt and my brother was adopted in 1968. His name is Jeffrey Phillip (after my grandfather) and he was my best friend from day one. After they got my brother Jeff, they decided to add a queen to their family and I became theirs. *My Mama used to call me "Queenie" so I thought I'd add that!*

Now, I need you to pay special attention to the letter on behalf of my parents about adopting another child. It was written by a co-worker of my Daddy. I was born on September 9, 1970 in Jefferson County, Alabama. And, remember my immigrant Great-Grandfather became a US citizen IN THE SAME COUNTY?!? Not a coincidence!

March 4, 1969

Montgomery County Department of
  Pensions and Security
P. O. Box 2005
Montgomery, Alabama 36103

Dear Mrs. ▓▓▓▓

I am writing in support of the application of Mr. and
Mrs. Ken ▓▓▓▓▓▓, ▓▓▓▓ ▓▓▓▓▓▓▓▓ Road, for adoption
of a second child.

Mr. ▓▓▓▓▓▓ is a valuable employee of the Appleton Wire
Works and a personal friend. I have known him and his
parents for 14 years. He is in charge of the electrical
operation of the plant, having worked his way up from
helper. This is quite a responsible position in a plant
this size, and he does an outstanding job.

Mr. and Mrs. ▓▓▓▓▓▓ are a devoted, home-loving couple.
Most of their activities seem to center around home,
church, and family activities. I would not hesitate to
recommend the ▓▓▓▓▓▓home as a suitable environment
for placing a child for adoption.

                            Very truly yours,

                            ▓▓▓▓▓▓▓▓▓▓▓▓
                            Manager
                            Montgomery Plant

jpd

Oh and this is very important...I was brought to them by a lady named Judy. (More about her later!). And, I will include a picture of my dad and I on my first day with them. You can tell that I loved him even on that first day!

I grew up always knowing that I was adopted. Once, when I was about 5, my brother was asking my mother about adoption and what it meant. I remember this like it was yesterday! I spoke up and told a story of a "Mama" tree that had a bunch of leaves and when the leaves fell off, they went to live somewhere else and were taken care of and "looked over" by some other tree. (Be looking for a children's book called the "Mama Tree" one day! I need to write this for sure!)

Having fun at the Lake with my Brother

I "GOT" the meaning of adoption even that young. I understood it even back then and like I said before, that "seed" planted way back was growing. I remember playing with baby dolls and I would line them up and pretend we were in church. I knew which babies were adopted and which babies were "out of my tummy." BUT, I loved them all the same. (Once again, adopted people will totally understand!)

Back to my mother. My mother was diagnosed with liver cancer in 2007. She beat it one time, but when it came back a second time, there was no mercy. Cancer is awful and doesn't let up. Liver cancer was cruel to my mother. I didn't realize how much the liver affects the mind. When the liver does not work properly, ammonia builds up and it causes dementia like no other. Onc day my mom would want to "shop until she dropped" and then the next day, she could not remember how to use the restroom. It also caused her to be argumentative and it was very upsetting to all of us. My mother ended up staying 14 days in Atlanta at Piedmont Hospital (THE BEST!) and I stayed with her the whole time. Then, we made the decision to bring her home to Montgomery and call in Hospice. My brother and I stayed with her every minute until one day I felt this overwhelming urge to go home. I felt so torn, but I had been away from my family for a long time and missed them and my home. I am a "smell-er " and I needed to "smell" my home. (For those of you who are ` "smell-ers" you will understand how those smells trigger you and can cause a flood of memories and even bring you peace!)

I left my parent's home with hospice there and my brother in charge. I told him I wanted to go home and be with my family in my home and sleep in my own bed. I was exhausted and felt that this would "re-charge" me for the rest of the fight my mom had left. I got a call the next morning from my brother. He told me that I did not need to rush to get there. I knew immediately that he was telling me my mother had passed away. I felt this complete feeling of guilt and it rushed in and I physically hurt because I had left my mother in her last hours. Guilt, in my mind, is equal to cancer. It Is cruel and can destroy you. I later found out that my cousin Marcia, who was more like my mother's best friend, had rushed to see Mama that morning because "something" told her to go and see her and she died shortly after Marcia was

13

able to see my Mom. No doubt that was Holy Spirit telling her to go see my mom. (Marcia is Ruth's daughter...Ruth was my grandfather's sister.) That morning was rough because I was still feeling guilty about leaving my Mom. On top of having to go pick out a casket, write the obituary and plan a funeral, that was a lot to deal with UNTIL my friend Lori told me that she felt that my Mom was waiting for me to leave and that if I had been there when she passed away, it may have been to difficult for me. And that maybe she felt that my Mom would have wanted me to be with my children when they found out. Those few words from Lori brought the end to my feeling of guilt and gave me peace at this sad time. You see, Lori had lost her dad already and she had been through losing a parent, so she said words to me that I needed at that time. (Important...Lori's dad's anniversary date of his death is the day before my mother's. So, we have each other to lean on during that week every December. As sad as that time is, it is easier every year knowing I have a friend feeling the same feelings & we have each other to face it every year. What a gift to help with that time in our lives!)

"He sets the time for birth and the time for death, the time for planting and the time for pulling up..." Ecclesiastes 3:2. GNB

Me with my Mama at my Wedding

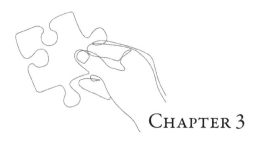

My Dad, Appleton
and Sadness

NOW THAT I have talked about my Mama, I need to tell you a little about my dad. Kenneth Scott was born on September 10, 1939 in Appleton, Wisconsin. He lived there most of his young life. My dad had a sister named Sandra, who passed away when she was young from an illness. He also has two brothers, and they both lived with us at different times when I was growing up.

My dad's father was named Al. His actual name is Albert Wilheim (cool middle name, huh?) Al met and married Dorothy Krause and they began their life in Appleton, Wisconsin. Like I said earlier, they had a daughter that passed away when she was young. I cannot even imagine having to go through that. And, for my dad, I know it has to be hard on him.

My grandfather worked for Appleton Wire Works and got transferred to the south to work at the plant in Montgomery, Alabama. I am sure that it was a huge change for their family. But, that change is what brought my parents together. They met at Lee High School in Montgomery. God had plans for these two to become one.

My dad was very good at basketball when he was in high school. He has several newspaper articles written about him and one article said that he had "ice water running through his veins" when he played. After high school, my dad realized he was good at working with machinery. He started his own business in 1974. He is brilliant when it comes to manufacturing and the company has grown tremendously.

17

My dad always took us on trips. We went to Disney World several times, we went camping, and went to the mountains several times. Lots of great trips gave me lots of great memories. (Matter of fact, on one of those trips, *I met Michael Jackson!)*

My Dad and I celebrating Father's Day

One thing that I learned as an adult was that my grandmother, Dorothy, my dad's mother, had suffered from depression. Back then, mental health was not discussed at all. You were considered to be "crazy" and looked upon like a fool. So, she suffered silently. Suffered so that she took her own life. Her death was never addressed or discussed. I think that my dad and his brothers were supposed to act like it had never happened. I honestly don't think my father has ever grieved her death. It does seem like every Mother's Day, for as long as I can remember, that he seems a little sad. I imagine that he is and it is okay to be sad. The grieving process is so important in the steps to heal. If you don't grieve, you can't heal.

The lesson I learn from all of this is you never should suffer in silence. Ever. And it is hard to imagine why the Lord would allow something that is so sad to even happen. But, God sees so much more than we do and He wanted Dorothy to come home to Him.

"If you do that, God will give you peace in your minds. That peace is so great that nobody can completely understand it. You will not worry or be afraid, because you belong to Christ Jesus." Philippians 4:7

My Parent's Wedding Picture with their Parents

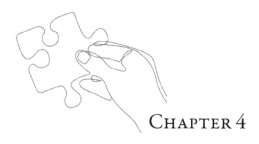

CHAPTER 4

LIFE-CANDY AND LIFE-CANDY KIDS

I SHARED A bit about my parents, but let me share a bit more about me. I grew up in Wetumpka, Alabama but I went to school at Alabama Christian Academy in Montgomery. ACA is a small, private school that was about 20 minutes from where I grew up. I started there in kindergarten, graduated there and I loved going to school there! I had some great teachers and am still close to several of them. Some taught me life-lessons and I am forever grateful for that school.

If it was not for ACA, I would not have my "Squad" of friends that I still have today. The friends I made there are life-long friends. One of my first friends that I met there is Abbie. We were in first grade together and she would always say that if she could look in the window at school and she could see my hair sticking up, then she knew it was going to be a good day! (I had short hair and I was so mad when I got it cut! It stuck straight up on my head most of the time!) We had the best time and the kindest teacher, Miss Blackwood. Miss Blackwood made such an impression on me and she even came to my wedding! And she keeps up with Abbie and me and is always posting a memory or saying something encouraging on social media to this day! Abbie and I have so many wonderful memories growing up together. She was always my friend and still is! Her mother used to say to us, "Have a happy heart!" Abbie makes my heart happy for sure!

On to junior high…I met another friend, Hayden. Hayden was so fun to be around and had the BEST CLOTHES! She would let me borrow anything to wear and we had so many fun times together…still DO! Hayden is my "mother hen." She is always taking care of me and makes sure I am where

I need to be! And her faith blows me away! Hayden, Abbie and I graduated together and are still "doing life" together. Hayden has a *calm-ness* about her that I see as strength. She is so loyal and loves me, genuinely loves me.

And then there is Gena. I met Gena when I was in the seventh grade. She is the grooviest friend I have. She came up with the expression "life-candy" and she is the definition of that. She is such an encourager and loves all of the music that I love. (Hang tough Children!)She always seems to say the perfect words that I need to hear at the perfect time! She is very thoughtful and one thing that I love about her is that she makes a point to send hand-written notes. No one does that anymore. Does anyone not feel 100% joy when you get a hand-written note? I think I have saved every single one she has ever written to me!

I am mentioning my friends because I want to share what a blessing having them is in my life. We make a point to be together, laugh, EAT and truly enjoy each other. They fill my cup! And most importantly, if I need prayers, these ladies will pray! Honestly, I do not know how I would survive without the encouragement they all give me. Three of us have lost our moms. Two of us have lost both parents. We have cried with each other through these losses and held tight to each other. Hayden has both of her parents. "Paul B and DD" have become all of our parents too! What a blessing it is to have them still! They are both very special and have loved me all of my life, during the good and bad times. They have never treated me any different since the day I met them. We often ask DD for advice and boy, she can give the best words that are TRUE!

Me, Abbie, Hayden and Gena

And, here is an even bigger gift...*our husbands and all of our children are friends.* Our kids all grew up together. We did birthday parties, Christmases, family trips and all of our kids know who "Their Tribe" is and have been in each other's weddings, and support each other. Some of our sons have all lived together in college and all of their children accepted and loved our Josh as soon as we adopted him. They loved him like he had been a part of "Our Tribe" all along. (More about our adoption to come!) All of our kids know that they have four "mamas" who love them and pray for them. I love to think about how much God must love our tribe. And he does. *He is so kind.*

Our Friends who are really Family!

Now on to Kelly, who is a ROCK! (The pajama story Kelly!))She is faithful and loves me! She also loves my children and they adore her. She is "Aunt Kelly " and we all love her. Kelly and I grew up together at church. Her parents were leaders at our church and her dad was an elder. They were always a source of stability for me and truly loved me, even though I was far from perfect! So basically they were true Christians. Her parents have both passed away, but their legacy and kindness will always live in my heart. Kelly is actually a GOLDEN ROCK! I will never forget Kelly sitting on the edge of my Mama's bed the night before she died. She was holding her hand singing "Trust and Obey." GOLDEN ROCK!

Me with my precious friend Kelly

I am also blessed with other friends that have been there for me in my life. Wendy, who is the friend that is just "easy." There is no stress with her and she literally would support me and love me no matter what! Wendy was "that friend" that literally went to the funeral home with fingernail polish and lipstick to put on my mother before her funeral because she knew what my mama would have wanted. (And she got the colors exactly right!)

My sweet friend Wendy

Now, Let me talk a little bit about Candace. (Because she is a "little bit." Tiny!) I met Candace at church and she is one of the hugest servants I know. She did volunteer office work at our church for a year with no pay. *A year. No pay.* What a servant heart she has! And...I got the opportunity to see her be baptized, which, in the picture that I have of that day, she looks like a baby, which reminds me of how we need to be more like children in our walk with Christ. Every once and a while, I will look at that picture just to remind me that I need the "fire" of being a new Christian back inside of me.

Candace being Baptized by our Pastor Wes with her Husband and Children watch

Everyone needs a friend like Karen, who will drop everything, pick up your girls and drive them to Atlanta when you are with your Mama at the hospital, just because you miss them. She is the friend who has showers and parties at her house for your kids just because she loves them like her own. And everyone needs a Cheryl, who listens, encourages and serves others by going the extra mile. She also is wonderful to talk "deep" with and gives "free therapy! She would be rich if she charged for her therapy! Everyone needs a Terri (with an I), who loves you and loves purple, and a friend like Terry (with a Y) that guides and mentors you! And you certainly need a Lisa, who always was my friend and always will be, no matter what! And let me add Patsy, who listens and is an example of making "lemonade when life hands you lemons."

There is also Patrick. He is my best and longest life-friend. He has been my friend for as long as I can remember. He is the kind of friend that you can call on at any time to help and he will practically jump to do it. We have been through a lot together. He was in my wedding and I had to be sure he was standing on the stage close to me. He is like my brother and will be even in heaven! Oh, I raise chickens(remember my vacations on the farm and I loved those eggs?) and he has helped me build pens, feed them, and anything else I need and *even get rid of snakes*! He is the kind of friend that will come to my house at 5:30 am to take my dogs out when I am out of town and worried about them. He is gold. And, he has been married for one year and his wife Jannette, is my new friend, and she arrived at the perfect time! I am loving getting to know her and see their love grow. She is so kind and creative (reminds me of my Mama).

My BFF Patrick & Precious wife Jannette - My favorite picture of them!

Each and everyone of my friends are a gift, and God gave them all to me.

I am going to stop right here and only mention the name of one of my friends. Her name is Margaret. God brought me Margaret (or Marge) just when I needed her in my life. There is more about her later on.

I could go on and on with my list of friends, but the reason that I am speaking of friends is I want to encourage you to hold friends close to your heart. You need those people in your life that are "life-candy." You don't need a large group of friends, you just need enough to surround you, be there for you, "do life" with you and love you for who you are. And, most importantly, pray for you AND pray for your children.

My parents have also had life-long friends, and that made them automatic friends of mine. The Holmes, Hendersons, Pate families and Anne G. have played huge roles in my life along with many others. They have loved me since the day I became a part of my family. I am sure that they have prayed for me and my family too.

When I think about friends, I think of these songs. (Sing along!)

"You've got a friend in Me" (Toy Story)
"I'll be there for you" - Friends TV show
(I am sure Gena likes all of these songs because I do. And "Purple Rain":)

Proverbs 18:24 "...But there is a friend who sticks closer than a brother."

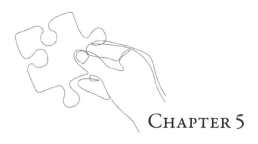

CHAPTER 5

THANK YOU LYNN AND
THANK YOU BASEBALL!

NOW, I NEED to let you know about another friend. Well, he is actually more than a friend! It is my husband Darrell. He truly was sent to me because the Lord knew what I needed. He was born in Pittsburgh, grew up in Arizona and ended up in Montgomery to play baseball at Auburn University in Montgomery. The CRAZY thing about how we met is amazing to me to this very day! We both had signed up for a broadcasting class. The class did not have a teacher and was cancelled. A lady who worked for our local news station stepped up and offered to teach the class. Her name was Lynn Sansom. (I recently located Lynn and thanked her!) We met in that very class and the first day I met him, I looked at my friend Cissy and told her, "I think I may marry that dude." I was right! It was only two months before we told each other we loved each other. And I never looked back! I knew he was the one and I wanted to start our life together. I have such great memories of him proposing to me! He blindfolded me and drove around all over town and then went to a neighborhood park that had a gazebo and lights. He got down on one knee and of course I said YES! I know that every step of our relationship was a perfect plan because my fiancé was born in "the Burgh", came from Arizona and we met in a class that wasn't supposed to be! Wow!

I sometimes think about what may have happened if that class was cancelled. Would we have met? Fell in love? God had it all lined up for us to meet. No doubt. Even though I didn't feel very good about myself, *God loved me enough to send someone who felt good about me!*

Darrell and I married in November of 1994. We had a beautiful wedding and recently watched our wedding video. Darrell's Uncle Carmen was one of the pastors at our wedding and hearing his sweet words from our wedding is so special to me. The words he spoke over us at our wedding mean so much to us and the influence Uncle Carmen and Aunt Elaine have had in our lives is so great. They were Darrell's family here in Montgomery, along with his cousins CJ and Rachelle, and they were the reason that Darrell even visited here and ended up playing baseball here. So you see, *they played a part in our lives even before Darrell and I met*. Uncle Carmen and Aunt Elaine loved and accepted me from day one!

Darrell has an incredible family. FUN ITALIAN FAMILIA! This is gonna sound like I am bragging and obnoxious, but they love me. I mean they *really love me*. They have accepted me from day one! My mother-in-law has always been so welcoming and whenever she introduces me to someone, she calls me *her* daughter. My father-in-law is wonderful to me and is a wonderful grandfather! I have made many wonderful memories with my FUN ITALIAN FAMILIA and what a blessing they are!

My Italian Family! Amo la Mia Famiglia!

I am also blessed with a special family member that is truly a bonus "mom" in my life. My brother-in-law's Mama Carol is so good to me and my family. She is my children's "MeMe" and really allowed my children get to still experience another grandmother when my Mama passed away. She is the one I go to for recipes and advice.

And, my sister-in-law Deneen is one of my best friends. We both laugh because we know she loves me more than she does her brother. We talk about so many things and I love our relationship. She is my sister. She has also accepted me for who I am from day one.

This is one of my FAVORITE pictures of my sweet Deneen!
Look at those beautiful brown eyes!

"Look at how good and pleasing it is when families live together as one." Psalm 133:1

Our beautiful wedding

"We love because God first loved us." 1 John 4:19 GNB

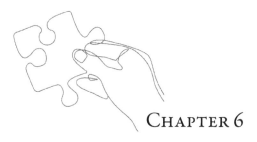

CHAPTER 6

Loss and Gain(s)

DARRELL AND I had a wonderful first year of marriage and truly enjoyed each other. We bought our first house in that year and knew it was time for our family to expand. We decided we would start trying for a baby. It didn't take long and before we knew it, we were expecting our first child. I was so excited and I could not wait until our baby arrived! We told our families and everyone was thrilled! I was due on June 22. My sweet sister-in-law Deneen and brother-in-law Tony already had a sweet little baby girl and we got lots of "parenting practice" with her.

I felt pretty good during my pregnancy. Darrell was still playing softball on a league team and we went out of town for a softball tournament. We took my cousins, Alex and Virginia with us. (They were also our "pretend children" and we loved taking them places with us!) On the trip, I started feeling strange. I knew something was not right. After the last game, the team and families went out to eat. I went to the restroom and it was confirmed that something was wrong. I had started bleeding. I was in shock and I remember shaking telling Darrell what was going on. I also had to pretty much "fake it" and act like nothing was wrong because I did not want to upset my young cousins. We had about a 3 hour drive home and I was able to go to the doctor the next day. The doctor ordered an ultrasound and it was confirmed that I had miscarried. We were devastated. Darrell called our families to let them know. It was so difficult to comprehend what was even happening. I could not understand how God could let this happen to us. But then it hit me and I thought that I may have lost the baby *because I had deserved it.* Now I know better. For anyone who has experienced a miscarriage, you know the feelings you experience. It is a loss with no explanation of why it happens and no way to explain how you feel. I feel like possibly the only reason that God allows this is so that we may help others if they have one. I know that when it happened to me, so many people who had experienced the same thing, said the most comforting words. I have always known the verse in Proverbs that says "Gracious words are a honeycomb, sweet to the soul and healing to the bones." I never knew the truth of that verse until I experienced a miscarriage, but that verse has shown true in my life many times since then.

I ended up having to have surgery that same day and I went home feeling lonely and empty. I also felt I was being punished by God and he would not allow me to have a baby.

Darrell and I went back to the doctor a few weeks after the miscarriage and my doctor was a huge encouragement. He said we should try again! Darrell and I both agreed to go for it and try again. In about four months I was pregnant again. Immediately my doctor took every precaution and did an ultrasound right away. I was lying there during the ultrasound and I heard Darrell start laughing. (He could always see things on an ultrasound better than me!). The ultrasound tech, who was the same ultrasound tech that we had for the miscarriage, said, "Julie, were you on fertility drugs?" I was like, "huh?' She then proceeded to tell me that there was AT LEAST two babies. Again, I was like, "huh?" And Darrell kept on laughing. We found out that we were having twins! They were due on June 24. (Remember, the baby we lost was due the year before on June 22?). God was giving us two babies right around the time we lost the first. WOW! *He loves me so much!* I begin to think that the miscarriage was not pay-back from God.

Christian (named after Darrell's best friend) Phillip (named after my grandfather and brother) and Ashleann (Ann after my Mom and also me) were born on June 4, 1997. What a joy! I was so happy to have them both and I love them dearly. They were both born healthy at 37 weeks. Christian was born first and weighed 6 lb 1 oz and Ashleann weighed 7 lb 11 oz. They were 47 minutes apart. (Yes, 47 minutes. That was the longest 47 minutes in my life!)

There are so many wonderful things about having twins. They were instant best friends and share a special bond. They are both so different. I tell so many people that I should have named them "Night and Day!" A funny thing that I got asked over and over (and over) is if they were identical. I still giggle at that question. (Boy/Girl twins are not identical and can never be identical. Hee hee!) They are wonderful and I adore them!

Now, let me introduce you to Emily Grace. She was baby number 3 for our family! She was born April 20, 2000. So we had 3 under 3 all at one time! But it was such a great life! We did not find out if Emily Grace was a boy or a girl and it was a wonderful surprise that she was a girl! This beautiful baby girl was 10lb 5 oz and 3-1/2 weeks early! (Funny story...when she was born, the doctor said, "Well, your baby is a girl and a toddler!)She was the best baby and was so entertained by her Bubba and Sisi. I honestly don't remember her ever really crying about anything. She was so happy and loved everyone. She also loved her pacifier, which I can thank Hayden for finally getting her to give it up! What a joy she is! We have a great time together! She is my concert-bud and we have seen several concerts and have many, many more to go to in the future.

When I look back and think of the kids being little, I can't believe how fast it has gone by. You literally blink and they turn one, then they start kindergarten, then they turn ten, then they start driving, then they leave you and go off to college. College is one thing that I hate. *I still hate it.* College equals heartbreak to me. I know that children need to grow up and "get an education" (which seems to be what society thinks), but parents with young children, let me tell you something, the day your children refer to somewhere else as HOME is totally a jab straight in your heart.

Ashley is married to her love Evan. Evan is an answer to prayer. Christian is married to his love Carley. Carley is an answer to prayer. Attention all parents! Start praying for your child's spouse TODAY. God answers those prayers. I have proof. And God will answer my prayers for two more!

Christian graduated from Troy University and is currently employed at Troy. He wants to work for Disney and would be thrilled to do that! Ashley is a dental assistant and in school for dental hygiene. She only has a few more classes and then boards and she will be finished. Emily Grace is currently in school at Troy University and is in marketing. She has a few more years left and wants to go into Fashion. She is a fashion queen! And then there is Josh. My cutie-pie Josh is awesome! We adopted Josh in 2013. What a JOY he is! That child has taught me more in my life about unconditional love than anyone else! He has a story to tell about his life and one day it will surely be his testimony! So many prayers have gone up for him! **UPDATE - CHRISTIAN AND CARLEY ARE DISNEY EMPLOYEES AND ASHLEY IS A DENTAL HYGIENIST! AND...I AM GOING TO BE A GRANDMOTHER! WOO HOO!

"Children are a gift from the LORD; they are a real blessing."
  Psalm 127:3

Me with the Kitty, the Lion and the Bumble Bee

Ashley and Evan with my Brother, Sister-in-law, Dad and Niece at their Wedding
***Ashley wore my dress I wore in my wedding, which was also
the dress my mother wore in her wedding***

Christian and Carley and our Family at their Wedding.
Carley wore her mother's dress at her wedding

I always like to show this picture off...The top is me with my "adopted babies" and the bottom is me with my real babies!

CHAPTER 7

NUDGE AND BUTTER STICK

THERE ARE SO many incredible details about our whole process in adopting Josh. The first one is that I felt the "nudge" of adopting a child way before Darrell did. Actually, back in 2009, we had the opportunity to sponsor a child from Malawi through our church. There was a table full of folders that had a child's picture and information about the child. We *chose* one and his name was Ronald. For many many years, we wrote letters to him and got updates on Ronald. We considered him to be family. Earlier, I spoke of us going to Malawi in 2013. *We got the opportunity to meet that precious Ronald face to face! Many prayers were answered that day!* I still consider Ronald to be my son and we communicate a lot! I truly love that fella! He has a huge faith and I love that about him! And I LOVE that he calls me MAMA! I believe that the "seed" was planted about us adopting through the opportunity to sponsor and love Ronald!

The WONDERFUL day we met Ronald in Malawi

Back to my Josh...We were approved to adopt and waited almost two years. I was so impatient. I am embarrassed to admit it, but it is the truth. I wondered how come we had not had a child placed with us when there were so many children who needed a home. Well, God knew that we had to wait on Josh! Josh became legally adoptable at the perfect time! It was in 2013 AFTER we returned from Malawi. He moved in with us in December and his legal adoption "Gotcha" day is May 5, 2014 - Cinco de Mayo! That day is double special because another family, who went through all of the classes and adoption process with us, celebrates their child being adopted that day also! Same courthouse & same judge! (AND, he was born in the same county I WAS!)

And, I actually need to go back a bit about Josh. Josh was born in October. That was the same exact week that our family moved into our house because we **needed more room!** We didn't know at the time that the extra room would be for Josh! And, I mentioned Judy earlier. Judy was the social worker that brought me to my parents. She also was the social worker that ended up doing our home study to adopt Josh! I know. It is unbelievable! But...God!

Josh is an incredible young man. He has been such a blessing. He is in the 7th grade and so handsome! She was very young when she had him. I am so thankful for her and that he is mine. He was in five foster homes before he came to us. And like I said earlier, *one day his story will be his TESTIMONY!* By the way, Josh was born premature. He was only 1lb. 8 oz. I tell him all of the time that he is my little "stick of butter." He is one handsome fella and I cannot imagine life without him and cannot remember life before him!

I mentioned earlier that I felt that "nudge" to adopt before Darrell did. It took several months to get him on board. He always encourages others that if your wife has the desire to adopt, then husbands need to be open to at least considering the idea. He is a great father and the kids love him! It has been so neat to see Darrell's and Josh's relationship grow. They are buds for sure and they make each other laugh and that is a beautiful sound!

Another cool Josh fact. Most kids when they are born do not get to pick out their own name, but before the adoption court hearing, Josh picked out a new middle name for him. He is Joshua Julius! (Julius is my dad's grandfather and I was named after him!)

> "God had already decided that through Jesus Christ he would make us his sons and daughters - this was his pleasure and purpose." Ephesians 1:5

Josh's adoption day - Cinco de Mayo! Can you tell that he
had an ARMY of people who already loved him?
***Josh loves the song "Masterpiece" by Danny Gokey. The words are perfect*
for my Josh. God is making a masterpiece in him!

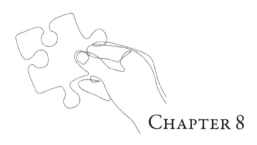

CHAPTER 8

BONE MARROW, LIQUID GOLD AND CANDY

NOW I KNOW you are looking at the title of this chapter thinking one of two things. The first being that when you hear bone marrow it usually means bad news. The second is "What in the world is liquid gold?" And I know you want to know what Candy has to do with it?

This part of my story isn't so much about me, it is just about how I experienced GOD WORKING!

I mentioned Evan, my son-in-law earlier. Shortly before I started writing this, we got some bad news. Evan's sister had been diagnosed with Leukemia. She is only 26, newly married and went to the doctor for a checkup. Her and her husband Adam had just found out that they were expecting a baby. She went in for the checkup and got very bad news. She was told that she had leukemia and was to go directly to the hospital. She also got the news that they had lost the baby. It was devastating to everyone. I remember my daughter calling me and she was bawling her eyes out.

Ava was told she had to go through some tough treatments. I honestly don't think it even hit her that she had lost the baby. I don't think her brain could process all of the news at one time. And let me add this, her and her husband live ten hours away from her family. And let me also add that this happened all during the COVID-19 pandemic. So, Ava had to face this all alone. Her husband could not be with her, her mother and father could not either. *She faced all of the treatments alone.*

I think I would have literally rolled up in a ball and shut down. I have thought so many times that she is so strong! One thing that I want to add is that from *Day One* in their marriage, they have honored God and welcomed Holy Spirit into their lives. I believe that this is what helped get them through this.

On to the "Liquid Gold" part of this. And it is GOLD.

During Ava's treatments, the doctors wanted to do a bone marrow transplant. They sent out tests to her family and my son-in-law Evan was a perfect match. It is very odd that a perfect match is found on the first test, *but he was*. They went to Ohio where Ava was for more testing and he was found to be a 100% match. The date for the transplant was set. Ashley and Evan came back home until time for the procedure.

I didn't know much about bone marrow transplants, but they are amazing. The person getting the transplant will change slightly into the person who donated the bone marrow. Ava is fair skinned, Evan will tan. Ava's skin tone may change. Ava may even start to crave the same foods that Evan likes. Amazing!

The day finally arrived and it was time for the bone marrow transplant. I had several family members praying for the procedure to go well. I texted everyone to let them know it had started. Right then, my cousin, Rachelle texted me that she was praying for Evan's bone marrow to literally be like *"liquid gold"* to Ava. Well, if you'd like to see how gracious God our Father is, keep reading. After the procedure, the doctor came to my daughter and told her that she had never seen bone marrow like Evan's. That his marrow was almost triple the number it was supposed to be. LIQUID GOLD! And, let me add that he and Ashley were able to make it to Ava's room to see her get the last of Evan's marrow by IV.

God is so good to us. Ava is 100% free of leukemia cells as of now.

I also want to mention this part, the Candy part. You may be hoping I am only going to talk about chocolate or something like that, but this is just as sweet!

Candy is my daughter-in-law's mother. She is so sweet and I am happy that we are able to be in each other's lives and it is all because of our kids falling in love! Right before their wedding, Candy was having a routine test and it was found that she had cancer. It was very upsetting and I will never forget the day that my sweet daughter-in-law Carley called to tell me the news. Everyone was in shock! We were also afraid because the wedding was coming up soon and no one wanted Candy to be sick. (And unfortunately, this was 2020, the Year of COVID, so we were also worried about her catching it! Which she did...we all did, but that's a whole story by itself!)

Candy was given the diagnosis of colon cancer and also breast cancer. My friend has made this journey being so positive and so brave! She has just finished her chemo for the colon and still has more breast chemo to go, but she is FULL OF JOY! She has smiled bravely through it all!

So, in my life, *at the same time*, my son-on-law's family and my daughter-in-law's family were all going through these cancer journeys. Both being so positive and an encouragement to me!

But, this is such a God thing...both of those families were praying for the other. And like I said, both of these ladies faced all of this with such strength and FAITH in Jesus!

> "For you created my inmost being, you knit me together in
> my Mother's womb. I praise you because I am fearfully and
> wonderfully made..." Psalm 139:13-14

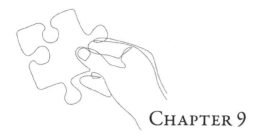

CHAPTER 9

BIO MOM & SURPRISE

I SPOKE ABOUT Josh's biological mom. Now I guess I should talk about mine. I will go ahead and answer the question that every adopted person gets. "Do you know who your biological mother is?" Yes I do.

I met mine by total accident. Well, I did do a little research to find out WHERE she was, but WHO she was was totally thrown in my direction. In 2007, my son Christian started doing the strangest thing and would throw up all of the time. I took him to the pediatrician and she did several tests to rule out the obvious terrible things. Praise God that all of his tests came back normal. I even took him to the eye doctor and he mentioned that it could be something genetic. I did not know any family history at all. The most information I had was written on a sheet of legal pad paper. I had read that adoptees could write in and get medical history if there was any in their file. So, I looked up how to do that and sent in a letter stating that *I only wanted medical history.* A week or so later, I got a letter in the mail from State DHR. I opened it and it was a birth certificate. I was so apprehensive reading it and then I discovered that it was *not* my birth certificate. The child on it was a male. So, I called DHR this time. I spoke with a gentlemen and told him what had happened. I told him *I only wanted medical records and no birth certificate.* He said he would only send medical information. A week later, there it was. My second letter from DHR. I was certain that it was only medical information. I opened it and there was not one piece of medical information in the envelope. Can you guess what was in there? *Yep. My birth certificate with my biological mom's name on it was staring me straight in the face.*

There it was, her name. I think I read it 100 times. I had no idea what to do with it. After a few weeks, I thought that obviously, the Lord wanted me to have this information. I didn't know why at the time. I had a friend who was a pro at finding information on people to help me out. He called me and gave me an address. I still didn't know what to do with this information. I had never felt like I *needed* to find her. But, here it was. So, I decided to send a message. I simply said who I was and asked her to send me any medical information, which she did. She sent a wonderful typed letter with both sides' medical history. After a few more letters and a phone call or two, we decided to meet.

Remember me talking about my friend, Kelly? This precious friend agreed to go with me to meet her. We met at a small country restaurant that was halfway between where we both lived. When we got to the restaurant, I sat down and had my back to the door. After a minute or two, I had the *urge* to turn around and at that moment, she was coming in the door. I knew instantly it was her. She sat down and seemed nervous. I was a bit nervous myself. (*note to any adoptee who is planning on meeting your bio parent...a restaurant is not the best place to meet. Meetings can be emotional, and every person at the restaurant can witness those emotions. I would suggest a large park, or some other place that is a bit more private.)

At our meeting, I found out that she had married my biological father 6 years after I was born and that *I have two siblings.* She has not told them about me as of today. It is hard for me to understand why she hasn't told them, and I feel like she is hiding me. I wonder if she is ashamed of me or afraid they will be ashamed of her. But, it is her choice. And I will honor that for now.

I remember staring at her. Staring at her face, staring at her eyes, and even staring at her hands. (Adopted folks, you get it, right?)

We have kept in touch a few times over the years. And a few years ago, my biological father passed away. I hate I did not get to meet him. And, I would have loved to see them together. I recently texted her to ask more about him and if he wanted to ever meet me. I am not sure if I am ready for the answer, either way.

BUT...an amazing thing happened regarding my biological family. Sit down for this one. We attend a small community church & I got our church email and saw that my friend Emily had lost a family member. The service was in the same town my bio parents lived in. Then I noticed that Emily's maiden name was the same last name as my bio father. Are you still sitting down? My friend Emily, that goes to my same church, who's daughters played on my Josh's soccer team, who also previously worked for Chikondi Health Foundation and had gone to Malawi, WAS MY BIOLOGICAL COUSIN. You cant make this stuff up. WOW! Another gift from Papa God. And to experience when we told her girls and my Josh that they were cousins, was priceless!

Maybe one day, I will meet more of my biological family. Maybe I won't. *Maybe is a good enough answer for me right now.*

I have a sister and brother out there. I know their names. I have seen their pictures and can see them on social media. It is strange, cool, unexplainable and indescribable all at the same time. Unfortunately, it stirs a sense of rejection.

I have learned through adoption classes that we took, that adoptees can hold on to that rejection. That it is felt even in the womb and starts there. It makes sense, that if there is an unplanned pregnancy, that words that are said, or emotions that are expressed are felt by the baby. If you are adopted, do you ever feel rejection? Do you "look" for rejection? Are you more sensitive to it? I highly recommend the "Trauma Prayer." (You can find this on the internet.) This can be for anyone who has experienced any type of trauma. But, this prayer asks that any thing that was experienced in the womb that would cause rejection to leave. And, it even asks if there are any smells that trigger trauma to leave. (For us "smell-ers", this is HUGE!)

I also recommend listening to the song "Wanted" by Danny Gokey. And if you have an entire box of Kleenex next to you, you need to watch the music video. Incredible, moving, and powerful are only a few words to describe it. I shared it with a very special person and they replied, "speechless."

"And we know that all things work together for good to those who love God, to those who are the called according to His purpose." Romans 8:28

*don't forget to watch the video ***with kleenex****

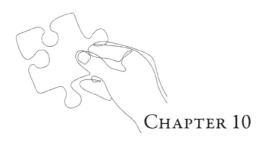

CHAPTER 10

BIO MOM & VERY UNEXPECTED UPDATE

IN THE PAST few months that I have been writing this, I had no idea that this would happen. I found out on social media that my bio mom passed away.

As I am writing this, there are many emotions that I feel. I am sad. I am hurt. I feel numb. I have questions...so many questions. And so many "what ifs" about this relationship.

When I found out, The funeral was the next day. I had thought that there would be no way that I would ever want to attend, but now I am second-guessing myself. Maybe it will bring closure. Maybe it will open up more wounds. I am really not sure.

Like I said before, I have two siblings. They have no idea that I exist. The one thing that I know is that I still feel like I need to honor my bio mom's wishes and not contact my siblings.

I went back to social media. I learned a lot about my bio mom that way. So many people posted such wonderful things about her. I smile as I read them. Seeing how many people she touched and how many children she taught in Sunday school was so wonderful to read. I saw that she had so many friends, including life-long friends that I am sure were her "life-candy."

It is the strangest thing to me. Reading all of this about a stranger, but it feels like I have known her forever. Part of me wishes I had seen her more and spent more time with her, while another part of me is okay with how everything was between us.

When reading her obituary, I read that her birthday was in March. March 4th to be exact. (Please take a minute to look back at the date of the letter written on behalf of my parent's to adopt me. There are also MANY significant things in my life that have happened in March!)

Now, she is in heaven with my Mama, and we will all be together one day.

I am sure that some of you probably read "Jesus Calling." If you do, you know that there are devotionals for every day with verses. My bio mom died on May 28. One of the verses for that day is Acts 17:28 which says, "...because God gives us life, we are alive. Because of Him, we can move about. Because of Him, we can be who we are...We too are God's children."

Thank you, biological Mom, for the choice you made to give me life. I am thankful for you.

Peace has flooded my soul. God gave me my life and everything is His plan. I am to be who I am SUPPOSED to be because of Him. I am His child. Nothing else matters.

> Psalm 136:1 "Thank the Lord, because He is good. His special love will always continue."

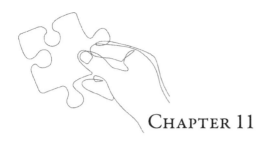

Chapter 11

My house, our home and a dream

I MENTIONED EARLIER that we moved into our house the first week of October, 2007. The same week that Josh was born, we moved into our house because we needed more room. We had no idea at the time what gift God was sending us. That gift was Josh whose birthday is the same week we moved into our home. The very same week! And it was six years later that he became ours!

I want to talk a little about my house. My dad built this house in 1972. He designed the layout of the house, where the bedrooms would be, how the den would look and, of course the basement where his business started. We moved in when I was two years old. I had a bedroom next to my brother and we shared a bathroom. We also had half of the basement to skate! My brother and I had our very own skating rink and I had many friends over to skate. Another part of the basement was an apartment my dad built for my grandparents when they were "in town." They lived at the lake, which is only 30 minutes away, but they would come and spend a night or two in their apartment. When they would come, it was like I had a mini-vacation. I would spend the night with them downstairs, but to me, it was as exciting as going on a trip! They would also spend the holidays and birthdays "in town"so every Christmas morning I got to be with my grandparents too as soon as we woke up!

Such good memories were made and are still being made in this house. I love the fact that I have been able to be with my family in the same house that I grew up in! That is not something that too many people get to experience!

When you read the title of this chapter, you probably thought that my house was my "dream home." I am happy here, but sometimes, my pride steps in and jealousy joins in too. You see, my house is as old as I am. We have updated some, but it seems as soon as I update something, it is time to update something else. I really have whatsoever-no-decorating-know-how and you already realized I am covered all up with ADD. So, needless to say, I struggle to not stress when people are coming to my house. Nobody cares what your house looks like, and I know that, but I kind of go into semi-panic mode. I need to work on opening up my home for friendship and fellowship. I need to pray about all of that, and I would appreciate all the prayers I can get.

You see, when I think, "oh, my house is so old" or "my house is not clean", or "I need to paint and get new flooring", my friends think, "I love her house" or "I grew up there" or "I have such great memories there" and "her house is so cozy!" But what I like the most, is that some friends have made it their home too.

You see, over the years, I have had several people stay at our house for a while. Whether it is because they need to "escape" their life for a bit, or a college student who needs a place to live during the summer. Or, one of my dear life-long friends went through a divorce and needed a place to stay with her kids and dog. She came to my home because this has been one of her "homes" growing up and feels safe here. What a blessing it is to know that people feel comfortable and safe here.

One of the greatest stories that was made between the walls of this house has to do with the "dream" part of the chapter title. It is an incredible story and could actually be it's own movie one day!

I have always had dreams that were very vivid. This dream was no different. I remember running around my neighborhood, (which is my neighborhood now). I was so upset and panicking because I could not find my friend. I kept calling out to my friend and no answer. I felt like my friend needed my help. I knew I had to find my friend. I kept running up and down the streets of my neighborhood screaming for everyone to help me find my friend. I kept reaching out my hand hoping my friend would grab on.

I woke up in a panic! I was so upset and knew I had to get in touch with my friend right away.

I called my friend as soon as the sun came up.

I got my friend to come over (by using another excuse) and right before they left I explained my dream and the panic that I had felt after having the dream.

My friend looked me straight in the face and said, "I do need your help. I am struggling right now in my life."

I want to keep confidentiality on this matter and this friend means the world to me, so I am being very vague on purpose.

I had no idea what all my friend was going through. It tore my heart out of my chest and the pain I witnessed my friend go through is something that I will never forget.

My friend felt comfortable in my home and I think it helped my friend make it through something that I don't think I would have survived. They felt PEACE here.

I feel that the Lord knew that I needed this home. Not just to raise my family in, but also to let people come here and stay where they are safe. To come to their "second home" to find strength and to heal. I also know that the Lord gave me that dream at the perfect time.

And, now the old saying, "Home is where the Heart is" has a whole new meaning.

> "Whoever dwells in the shelter of the Most High will rest in the shadow of the Almighty. I will say of the Lord, He is my refuge and my fortress, my God, in whom I trust." Psalm 91:1-2

Meaning of the word SHELTER - a place giving temporary protection from danger

Meaning of the word REFUGE - a condition of being safe or sheltered from danger or trouble

Meaning of the word FORTRESS - a person or thing not susceptible to outside danger or influence

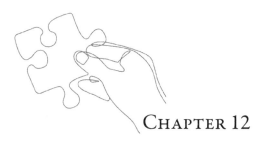

CHAPTER 12

THE WARTHOG, THE LINE
AND THE LESSONS

"NOW WHERE IS she going with this?" I know you are thinking it, and it is ok. It's how my brain works.

First off, the warthog. Have you ever seen one in real life? They are so incredible. I got to see them up close and personal on a trip to Africa. There they were minding their own business with hippos hollering in the background and I am just staring at them. You see, a warthog has to literally lean down on its elbows to be able to eat. So they will be walking around and the next second, they will "bow down"and eat. I couldn't help but think, "Now, why in the world would God make them have to bend down like that to eat?" I don't ever have to ask God that question, because I did a little research on my own. God did make them that way, BUT, God also gave them "special knee pads" that equip them with what they need. (Remember my Moses sermon story?) And, by the way, those jokers can run over 30 miles per hour!

Now, on to the LINE. I got the pleasure of riding out to our Mobile Clinic in Malawi Africa. If you are not sure what a mobile clinic is, I will explain. A group of people from Blessings Hospital in Malawi go out to nearby villages to treat patients every week. And when I say nearby, it is not the kind of nearby we know of. The one I went to took about an hour bus ride on what I thought were roads, but I wasn't quite sure. Ashley, who works for Chikondi Health Foundation and lives in Malawi, is the Nurse Practitioner that took me and my daughter, Emily Grace to this village. She explained that people lined up to get medical treatment there. Most of them are there for Malaria, which CHF treats them at no charge to the patient. When we arrived, I could not believe my eyes. There was a much longer line than I could have ever imagined. Some of them had walked for days, while sick, just to get medical attention. I realized how much I take for granted at that moment. If I am sick, I can go 15 minutes to my doctor, who is also my friend. Those people and that line are forever in my brain.

Another LINE that I experienced was the children at the orphanage getting a chance to pick out new clothing. On this day, they were only allowed to get 5 pieces of clothing. I watched those children pick their clothes out of a big pile of clothing that people had donated. It didn't matter what color, or if it even matched, they just got what was necessary. It also brought me to tears when I saw the older children pick only one or two things for them, and pick the rest for a younger child.

And, all of the lessons learned in Malawi...There are honestly so many that I could write a book on just Malawi. There was not a day that went by that I did not see something that drew me to Jesus. The scenery is beautiful and the people are beautiful, especially on the inside. They are kind and have faith that would move mountains. But the most valuable lesson that I learned there was that I went to Malawi with this idea that I was going to "help" these people. They were who helped me. It opened my eyes to so much that I needed to become.

"For God so loved the world..." John 3:16

If you want to learn more about Malawi and Blessings Hospital, or even want to join us on a medical mission trip, look at our website, on facebook or instagram.

www.Chikondi Health Foundation.org

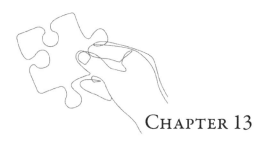

CHAPTER 13

A Sweet, Beautiful Baby & The Best Diaper Bag in the World

By now, you have probably figured out that the smallest things make some of the biggest impressions on me. This one, well, *this one is huge.*

Once upon a time, there was a beautiful baby girl born into this world and the Lord had huge plans for her life. But, way before she was born, she was loved. Loved from the minute that her parents found out that she was going to arrive and many, many prayers were prayed for this baby.

The mother found out she was expecting and knew she had to share this with the father. This is where the story seems different than you may expect. You see, the parents were very young. They mother was a senior in high school and the father was a junior. Both were seventeen years old. At seventeen, no one knows exactly what they are going to do with their life. You are trying to prove that you are responsible but at the same time, you need your parents to tell you what to do. It is an interesting time where you are trying to "soak up" all of the fun you can but be an adult at the same time. Seventeen is basically a "fork in the road" where you have to make decisions. And sooner than later, this couple would have a very difficult decision to make.

The mother told the father she was expecting. Like I said before, from the moment they knew the baby existed, the baby was loved. The baby was loved so much that they knew that they had to do what was best for her instead of thinking of themselves.

Time passed quickly. The mother graduated from high school and the father finished his junior year. Both were still seventeen with a baby on the way.

The day came for the baby to arrive. The mother was rushed to the hospital and in a few short hours, the baby made HER grand appearance! Yes, I said "HER"! The baby was a BEAUTIFUL baby girl. The mother took one look at her and knew right away she looked just like her, but had her father's eyes. She also realized that this may be one of the last times that she would see that baby's face. The mother spent as much time as she could with her until it was time to say goodbye. They were placing her for adoption.

If you look up the definition of goodbye in the dictionary, it means a parting, a final farewell but in this story, *it meant heartbreak.*

The mother went home. The father went home. The baby went to a different home, a foster home. But, the parents never stopped thinking of her, praying for her and loving her. And...stay tuned...so many of these prayers were answered!

When babies are adopted, they go to a foster home for about six weeks before placing the child with their forever family. This foster home is very special. They cared for the baby girl and loved her until she met her new Mama and Daddy. They also did a wonderful thing. When the baby came to their home, they were given information about the biological parents and they cut the lining of the baby's diaper bag and put the papers inside. They wanted the child to have this information because they knew how important it is to "know" for adopted children. So, a plain old diaper bag became such a special part of this baby's life forever.

Now on with the story...

Once upon a time, there was a beautiful baby girl born into this world and the Lord had huge plans for her life. But, way before she was born, she was loved. Loved from the minute that her parents found out that she was going to arrive and many, many prayers were prayed for this baby.

I know I started this with the same paragraph, but the same exact words about this baby can be said by the adoptive parents. They loved this child before they ever met her. And they were wonderful parents, the baby became a part of a wonderful family! She was loved so much! She had a wonderful life, wonderful friends and has a wonderful husband. (Here is the part where there is proof that prayers for her were answered!) Specific prayers that were prayed were ANSWERED for this beautiful baby girl!

And guess what? This beautiful baby girl had a PURPOSE!

> "For I know the plans and thoughts I have for you, says the Lord, plans for peace and well-being and not for disaster, to give you a future and a hope." Jeremiah 29:11

A message about fostering and adopting...

There are not nearly enough foster families and families who adopt. We certainly need more! BUT, we need good ones! Foster families that make a difference in the lives of kids and adoptive families that are forever families, are the ones we need. If this is something that you think you may be interested in, please contact me and I will be more than happy to connect you to the right people! If you feel that "nudge", DO IT!

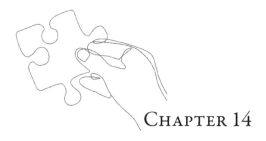

CHAPTER 14

WRESTLING, PAPA AND
HOME ECONOMICS

Weird. I know. You think I am weird. These chapter titles, I know. They are weird.

Have you ever watched wrestling? I used to watch it when I was young. Patrick and I would watch Hulk Hogan and Macho Man Randy Savage in the ring and were mesmerized by the action. And I even watched Dewayne "The Rock" Johnson and if you did, join in..."*Can you smell what the Rock is cooking?*"

Most people that know me would never in a million years think that I used to like wrestling. But, I have an awesome memory about wrestling that has nothing to do with any famous wrestler. It has to do with my first meeting with a very special man. A man I had no idea at the time, would have such an impact on my life.

Early on when I was dating Darrell, I was excited to meet his family. I already adored his mother, sister and my brother-in-law. Now, he wanted me to meet his Uncle Carmen and Aunt Elaine. They had invited us for dinner and we headed over to their home. When we got there, the WONDERFUL smell drifted out of their kitchen, straight up into my nose and I knew this would be a good night! I met Darrell's Aunt Elaine and I remember thinking that she was one of the most beautiful ladies that I had ever seen. I was given a huge hug by her and she told us to head on into the den where Uncle Carmen was sitting. When we got there, he jumped up, hugged me and sat back down on the floor. We talked for a while and he asked me all sorts of questions to get to know me. I couldn't help but let my eyes drift to the TV where he had wrestling on. (ADD, remember?) A bit later, Aunt Elaine called his name. He looked at Darrell and I and excitedly said, "Alright, let's go!" He kind of moved around on the floor and I just plopped down next to him in the "ready to wrestle" position. Darrell and Uncle Carmen both looked at me like I was crazy, but I thought he was challenging me to a wrestling match right there in his den. When he told me that Aunt Elaine was calling us to come and eat, we all busted out laughing, I was just going to go with the flow, but I knew immediately that I would ADORE them!

I know that I mentioned them both earlier in my story, but I don't think if I had one hundred pages about them it would be enough. These two influenced me more than I even realize. Uncle Carmen and Aunt Elaine taught me about grace, about being a true Christian, about rest, about racial-reconciliation, about the Holy Spirit, about the GIFT of Jesus, and (I LOVE THIS) about Papa God. Uncle Carmen referred to God as Papa God so many times and I just love the image of that. A big, ole, cozy Papa loving us. These two opened my eyes and my heart to so many wonderful things. I am so thankful for that.

Home Economics used to be taught in schools everywhere. I am not sure when or why this stopped. Every human should have Home Ec! I think Aunt Elaine could have written every textbook on Home Economics. She is superwoman when it comes to taking care of your home and everyone and everything in it. When we were at her home, it didn't matter if she fed just us or thirty people, there would be exactly enough and everything would be cleaned up shortly after we ate. She can sew anything and is just amazing. A few years ago, she took on the job of teaching our oldest three, along with my niece and nephew, home economics. They would go to her house and she would teach them all how to clean, cook, plan meals, sew and Uncle Carmen would add important lessons also. She instilled an idea of "serving others" to those kids and they loved spending time with them.

Aunt Elaine is also such an example of service and strength to me. Uncle Carmen was diagnosed with cancer and she served him until his last day and after he passed, she has shown such strength with her faith. Before he passed, she invited us to come to see him in his last days, one family at a time. I know that this had to be hard for her to witness, each one telling him good-bye. I remember every moment of the last time I saw Uncle Carmen. Aunt Elaine had us all go into the bedroom and she looked at me and said, "Crawl up there with him. He would love that." I did and the words he said to me spoke LIFE into my soul. He told me so sweetly, "*Papa God thinks you are perfect.*"

Words can be LIFE can't they? I honestly cannot even type all of this through my tears. What an honor it was to hear that from such a wonderful man, who was close to perfect in my eyes.

I have two verses for these two very special people.

> Romans 8.15 "...You should behave instead like God's very own children, adopted into his family - calling him, "Father (Papa), dear Father (Papa)"

> Proverbs 31:10-31 pretty much describes Aunt Elaine.

Uncle Carmen and Aunt Elaine
**Uncle Carmen also taught me about Body, Soul and Spirit. Incredible. He also has written a book on Amazon called "Dark Night of the Soul."

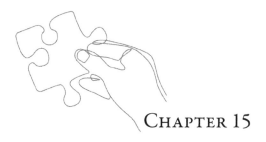

CHAPTER 15

THE DEER, TWO GUYS WITH AN "O" AND "YOU NEVER KNOW"

I LOVE HOW my chapter titles just keep getting better and better.

The first thing in the title of this one is a deer. Now, what in the world would make me write about a deer? Well, I have a pet deer. She is not caged or even around every day like my other pets. But, to me, she is my pet. I love to feed her and she knows she is safe with me. Her favorite thing to eat is bird seed and she loves when I cut up apples and bring them to her. She also has had several sets of twin baby deer that she brings around me every time she has them. This year, she had one of them in my backyard and one of them in my front yard. I finally saw the two together and they are precious.

I have named this sweet deer "Mama." She comes back to me so many times and she trusts me. (You may be asking me how I know that it is the same deer. Mama deer has a small notch on her ear. I noticed it years ago.)

I was sitting on my steps watching her and was amazed at how she keeps coming back to me time after time, year after year, and even wants to have her babies around me. I am sure that over the years there has been more than one occasion that I forgot to feed her or didn't think of her. But, she keeps coming back. Then it hit me. That Mama deer is like Jesus. He keeps coming back to me, time and time again. Even when there may be days where I don't put Him first, He comes back to me. And, has given me such wonderful things in my life. He shows those to me, just like Mama deer shows me her babies. She trusts that I will take care of her, just like we should trust Jesus because He will take care of me.

Now, on to the two guys with an "O." I promise that this will make sense. The first "O" is not a human. The first "O" is an Alpaca. His name was Albert-O and my friend Allyson was his owner. She raised him from a baby and that Alpaca thought he was human! He would sleep in a recliner, ride in her truck and just make himself at home in her home. Allyson used Alberto the Alpaca to spread joy. She would take him to events, vacation Bible schools, nursing homes, just anywhere that needed his joy. And people loved that little guy! You see, it doesn't take much to bring people joy, and this little Alpaca taught me that people need joy. I need to work more on spreading joy like Alberto and Allyson.

One Christmas, Alberto became sick. I can guarantee this, there has never been or ever will be an alpaca that had as many people praying for him than Alberto. Sadly, he passed away. Everyone was heartbroken, especially Allyson. But, guess what she did? She began using her other alpacas to keep spreading the Joy to others.

The next guy with an "O" is a co-worker at ISCI. His name is Robert, but I often called him "Robert-O." Robert and I have worked together since 1987 and he was one of my brother's best friends. They went on several trips together and made many great memories. Robert had pictures of these trips and would love to show you the pictures and tell you all about the details of their trips.

Robert was at most of our family gatherings. I laughed recently about this because I think he has experienced every family argument that we have ever had! He fit in with everyone in our family and he has a dry sense of humor. He let things roll off of his back easily and didn't ever seem stressed. He enjoyed life to the fullest and even took a trip on his Harley from Alabama to Niagara Falls. I am so glad that he got to take that trip.

Robert was another who spread joy. I never asked him if he was a Christian, but I know that he was because of his joy, and I think that you couldn't live like that if you didn't have Jesus in your heart. You never knew if he had a good day or a bad day, because he was smiling EVERY day! You would think that someone who smiled every day had a happy, perfect life. But, it was the opposite. You see, my friend Robert lost both of his parents at the same time. They left their home a few minutes before Robert and were both killed instantly in a car accident a few miles from their home. Robert was one of the first cars that came upon the accident.

Could you ever get over that? I mean, could you? I couldn't. I can't imagine the heartache he must have felt every day and every time he came up to the area where the accident happened. In an instant, his life had changed. Most people would be bitter, angry or sad most of their life. I know I would. But not Robert, he kept his joy.

Robert also had a heart attack several years ago. If it were me. I would be a nervous wreck that I would have another one. After he recovered, he truly enjoyed life. He had to have a pacemaker. Recently, he had an issue with it and was going in to have a minor procedure done to fix it. He never made it out of the hospital. We still cannot believe it. Our friend has passed away. Our friend who spread his joy, is gone.

My brother also has heart issues and stayed with Robert at the hospital. His heart began to beat "out of rhythm" and pretty much stayed out the whole time Robert was in ICU. Since Robert didn't have family, my brother helped make the funeral arrangements. I got a call from my brother and he told me that the minute he pulled away from the funeral home, his heart went back into rhythm. God calmed his heart at that very minute, and gave him peace. I believe it.

Here is the "you never know" part of my story. You see, at ISCI, about a month prior to Robert's passing, we lost another long time employee named Mike. Mike was also a joy, a very kind friend who never complained. He was usually the first one to arrive in the mornings and often, the last one to leave. Mike was another one who had not had things easy. He went through a time in his life where things happened in his family that I can't even fathom. (I am and will always protect his privacy.) But, he was joyful! No matter what day, or what time, or what was going on, you could depend on hearing, "Hey Buddy!" every time I called his office. He had worked with us for 30 years and also passed away unexpectedly. He was only 60.

You never know when it will be the last time you see someone. Make it count.

2 Samuel 22:34 "He makes my feet stand strongly on the ground. Like a deer, I can stand on high mountains and not fall."

CHAPTER 16

THE MESSAGE, THE BLESSING
AND HEALING

HAVE YOU EVER gotten a message from someone that made your day? Words that felt like a blessing and when you read them, you felt like you were on a path of healing and happiness? This message was just that and more.

If you are old and need to read an "IPhone for Dummies" book like I do, then you will totally get what I mean when I tell this part of the story.

A message appeared on the phone. She had no idea who it was from. It came in the way of social media and honestly, it was confusing to her how she could receive a message from someone she did not know. But there it was. Sitting there, waiting to be read. She clicked on this message fully expecting it to be about work or some type of scam message that needed to be deleted immediately. Instead, the message absolutely blew her mind. She read it and then dropped her phone. The feeling of shock came across her like it had never before. The message was simple and to the point. It simply said, "Hello. So this may be a random question, but does (date given at a later time) mean anything to you?"

Of course the date meant SO much to her. So, she answered this message with a simple "Yes" and a Purple Heart. (You'll have a whole different love for purple after this!)

The next messages that went back and forth went like this...

"I was worried I may have offended you by reaching out."
"Not at all. I actually prayed that you would one day."

"I have always wondered and hoped I could find you. "

And then there was this question...

"So what was the reason for giving me up?"

And then this...

"Well, I want to thank you. I have had a wonderful life."

Again, words can SPEAK LIFE, can't they? She immediately felt the past being washed away.

And then she answered with this message.

"From the first time I laid eyes on you, I prayed you would understand what I did. I have prayed so many prayers for you your whole life."

God answered all of those prayers. All of them.

Many, Many messages went back and forth between them. For months they "talked." Many questions were answered and a relationship between these two had blossomed. They both could not believe how much they were alike & how much they had in common!

There was also a lot of *healing* that came from these messages.

And here brings me to the "Purple Heart" part of the story. One asked the other in one of the messages about what her favorite color was.

The answer was purple for both.

And then this message.

"I knew it had to be you from your first message with a Purple Heart."

I told you that purple will have a whole new meaning for you. I hope you will think of this part of my story every time you see purple. I hope you think of grace, forgiveness and KNOW that God answers prayers.

"Every good thing given and every perfect gift is from above..." James 1:17

CHAPTER 17

THE MEETING AND THE MEETING

EVERYONE HAS MEETINGS that they have to go to. Some of them you can't wait to get to, some you dread, some you love and some you just go to because you have to. Meetings can be helpful, some not so helpful, long or short. Every person that reads this could probably tell their own story of a meeting that they experienced.

Once again, I looked in the dictionary to find an official meaning of the word "meeting."

Part of the definition says that a meeting means this…"a coming together of two or more people, by chance or arrangement." These are both by chance and arrangement.

In this part of the story, we will be talking about two meetings. I'll do my best to keep everything together for each part. (Remember, I have ADD!).

In the last chapter, I talked about the many messages that happened between two people. After a few months, these two decided to meet. It had been a long, long time that these two had been apart.

A date was set and they were going to meet! Everyone was so excited! So many emotions were felt by her on the drive there. When she arrived, there was a "Hi!" And then she answered, "Hello!" And, she was greeted by the hugest hug! She had so many emotions but it was comfortable. *Everything felt natural.*

She also felt like she was looking in a mirror. And it was amazing how much this woman looked like her other children. It was amazing how much she felt she "knew" her already.

Once again, God had answered prayers that she could meet her biological daughter one day. And that day was here. She felt like her heart would burst the first time she heard her voice. And that first hug, the first time they looked at each other eye to eye after all of these years was unreal, unbelievable and indescribable all at the same time!

Lots of conversation, lots of laughs and lots of food were a part of that day and every bit of it was great! It seemed like a dream! The daughter's best friend was there also. (And, someone actually videoed it all! YAY!)

The past was washed away.

The last sentence is an important one. Remember how important praying friends are in your life? One friend prayed those exact words over this meeting before it happened. He prayed that the past would be "washed away." And that is exactly how everyone felt. It felt like freedom.

The other meeting that will be a part of this story is a meeting that had to happen. She had to tell her other children about the person on the other end of the messages. They needed to know about this person on the other end of the messages. They had no idea and she had no idea how they would take the news.

Her greatest fear was that her children would think differently about her. That they may think of her the same way she had thought of herself. She felt for so many years that she was not worthy. She felt guilty. She felt awful about herself. And her greatest fear was that her children would think bad things about her. She had carried so much emotion around for so many years and she did not know if she would ever be able to share it. She had "trained" herself to keep it all to herself, to not share, to not hurt and to move forward. She had no idea on how to tell her children but knew that her past was part of her purpose.

There is no book, no podcast, no instruction manual to help people get through this and the correct way to do this. She was not sure how this had to happen, but knew it had to happen, sooner than later.

The meeting date was set and it arrived. She sat them down and began the story. It was very difficult for her to get through it and had a hard time finding the right words to say. It was very quiet and there was a lot of emotions shown. The kids were angry because she had kept this from them. But mostly, they were upset that their mother had carried this around for so many years. BUT, they all said that they didn't want her to feel guilty about her past.

She hopes one day they will forgive her and understand why she kept this from them for so long. Only God will heal them all.

But, It was out finally. And finally, *she could breathe.*

> "You will know the truth, and the truth will set you free." John 8:32

Chapter 18

Praise team and New Wine

Now, when you see the title of this part, you are probably thinking that since I wrote "Praise Team" that I can sing. Wrong. I wish I could, but I can't

This part is about one of my daughter Emily Grace's friend Kelsie. She has a beautiful voice and we encouraged her to try out for our church praise team. She finally got up the nerve and told me that her time to practice was an upcoming Wednesday night. We all went to her practice to hear her sing. I was excited and nervous for her, but since she had such a beautiful voice, I knew it would be great. She began to sing. The song she chose was "New Wine." I had never heard this song, but after I heard Kelsie belt it out, I loved it. I immediately went home and downloaded the song.

Have you heard it? It is beautiful. The lyrics are so powerful. Please find them, read them and *absorb* them.

Now that you have read the words, let them sink in.

I would play that song over and over and sing (with my not so beautiful voice) loud and proud.

I repeat. I would play that song over and over and sing (with my not so beautiful voice) loud and proud.

I had no idea how much this song would mean to me. And I had no idea that I was asking Jesus to bring crushing, pressing, surrender, new ground, power, freedom, for me to release old flames with new fire and to make ME HIS VESSEL.

And, what does it mean to be called HIS VESSEL? It means that you are a person who is a "holder" or "receiver" of something non-material.

I know now, I WAS CHOSEN BY GOD, to be a "VESSEL OF GRACE."

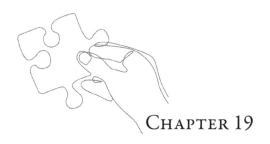

CHAPTER 19

FINISHING UP THE PURPOSE PUZZLE

Now, I BET by now you are feeling one of three things. You are probably either bored to tears and ready for this to end. You may be totally confused because you cannot follow my ADD way of thinking, or (hopefully) you are wanting to hang on and see how in the world this all fits together - like a big, CRAZY PUZZLE.

So, I will go back to the beginning. Remember my friend Terry, who had challenged me with the question, "What's your purpose?" I gave her my answer and hopefully, you can see my purpose also.

Me being a parent is not my purpose. My job is not my purpose.

MY PURPOSE IS THIS...

TO HELP EVERYONE KNOW THAT EVERYTHING IS IN GOD'S TIMING!

(I kind of gave a clue when I listed Ecclesiastes 3:1 as the first verse! I wasn't just quoting a line from Footloose. Ha!)

Basically, I have shared so many important things about my life staring with my great grandfather, my parents, my friends and all the way down to me and my children.

BUT, there is more to my story.

(Imagine me, right now, taking a huge, deep breath.)

I shared so much, but I need to share more. (And another deep breath.)

Let me go back a few pages to "The Message, the Blessing and Healing" part of my story.

Remember me talking about a message appearing on the phone? The message was for me. Let me repeat...THE MESSAGE WAS FOR ME. The message read, "Hello. So this may be a random question, but does *now is the time I fill in the date* September 22, 1988 mean anything to you?"

Are you putting the pieces together yet?

You see, I was the seventeen year old that found out she was pregnant.

I was a senior in high school and experienced more that year than some people do in a lifetime. (I was not the senior I talked about on page one that knew her purpose.)

I mentioned my friend Margaret earlier. I saved more info about her just for this part in the story. I grew up being a "Tom Boy" most of my life until Margaret arrived. I then had a girl as a best friend. I had no idea that all of those years growing up together how much I would depend on her during this time of my life. She was the one who went in the store to buy my pregnancy test and sat in the bathroom with me while I waited on the results. She was the one who encouraged me and even read several books on how to deliver babies in case of an emergency! God certainly sent her to me and I am so thankful for her and the important part she played in my life.

When I took the pregnancy test, I was in my bathroom at my house with Margaret. I took the test and waited until it was time and I remember finding out the results. It was positive. I was pregnant. This will seem strange, but I don't remember being upset. I didn't cry or think anything negative. I just knew I was pregnant and had a baby on the way. I know that some may think this sounds like I didn't care or was in denial. It was exactly the opposite. I accepted that I was pregnant and I think right at that very moment that I saw that plus sign on the pregnancy test, God was with me. It was a calming, peaceful feeling that came over me that caused me not to worry. He never left me and I realize it more now than I did then.

Being a senior in high school and seventeen I pretty much didn't ever think that the baby would arrive. I know that sounds absolutely insane but, once again, I had a seventeen year old brain. I thought I had all of the time in the world to figure things out. My senior year would soon pass by and the baby was coming.

Hayden's mom DD (the one with the good advice) came to me and told me that she knew that something was "up." She could tell that I needed someone to talk to and encouraged me to go ahead and tell my parents. My friend Abbie's mom Betty, actually made an appointment for me to go and see a doctor. You see, God knew that I would need those women in my life at this time, but put these friends in my life many years before. God is so good that way. He gives us gifts even way before we know why he gives us these gifts!

I remember telling my parents that I was pregnant. They were shocked, like any parent of a seventeen year old daughter would be. Then I told my brother. My brother gave me the biggest hug and told me he loved me.

Right before I had the baby, I turned eighteen. Not too many eighteen year olds get maternity clothes for their birthday presents. But, I did celebrate my birthday with my family, Patrick and Margaret.

I remember going into labor, but at the time, I didn't know it was labor. Because my Mama could not have children, she couldn't share any experiences of child birth, so everything I felt, I had no idea about. I went and woke my parents up and they drove me to the hospital. ("Do you remember the 21st night of September"? And I love that song!)

The next day, I delivered *alone*. Since I was eighteen, I was considered an adult. I was far from an adult at that moment. I was scared to death and knew no one. It seemed like a long, long time, but at the same time things seemed to move quickly.

SHE ARRIVED! The doctor announced I had a healthy baby girl! I immediately got to hold her. I remember looking down at her sweet face thinking that she looked so much like me, but had her father's eyes. I got to spend several minutes with her before they took her to the nursery for her checkup.

Every time the nurses came in to ask if I wanted them to bring her to me I said, "Yes!" I knew that my time with her was limited. I knew it wouldn't be too long before I had to tell her goodbye. I talked earlier about the meaning of goodbye, and *this was true heartache.* I said many prayers over this sweet, beautiful baby and finally the goodbye was here.

The nurse came into my room and told me that I was being discharged. I got dressed and felt a little lost. The nurse brought my baby to me one more time. I held her and told her I loved her. As hard as it was to leave, I knew the beauty of adoption. I knew that even though it broke my heart into a million pieces, that this was the best thing for her. *I just hoped she knew how she was WANTED and LOVED.*

You may be thinking, "How can she say that her baby was wanted and loved if she placed her for adoption?" I will try to explain the best I can. You see, I WANTED her from the moment I found out I was pregnant. I WANTED her to have her best life, and I LOVED her enough to put her before me. No matter how much it hurt.

I got home and physically ached because I missed her already. I had become that "Mama Tree" in the children's book that I am going to write one day.

I did my best to go on with life. You see, the same brain that made me think that the baby would never arrive was the same brain that *had me go forward and never look back.* I never really talked about any pain I was feeling, I just never looked back.

Recently, my friend Abbie and her husband Russ told me that they had thought that I was the strongest person they knew because I made it through giving my baby up for adoption. I don't think of it as "strength" but now I know that God helped me deal with my emotions and be strong, by not letting me look back.

BUT, NOW, I get to look back and see all of the prayers that I had prayed for this child come to fruition. She has had a wonderful life, with wonderful parents, wonderful life-candy friends and a wonderful husband.

PLUS, she has shown me the most wonderful GRACE and FORGIVENESS that I still wonder if I even deserve. I often tell people that God has given me this gift and I am not sure why because I don't feel I deserve it. OH! HE FEELS LIKE I DESERVE IT! HE IS SO KIND!

(Remember the "New Wine" song?) I am HIS VESSEL OF GRACE! BUT, SO IS MY BIOLOGICAL DAUGHTER! She could have been upset, angry, and not wanted to have anything to do with me, but she has shown me KINDNESS and given me such PEACE. I am so thankful for the woman that she is and the JOY she is! What a BLESSING! Not too many people get to actually receive a GIFT like I got and I have to share my story!

So, let's move on to meeting her again. It was a special day for sure. My husband Darrell was there by my side. We drove a little over an hour and finally arrived where we were going to meet. (And thank goodness it was not at a restaurant! - Remember my meeting with my bio mom?) I was so excited! Maybe a little nervous, but thrilled to finally see her face to face, hear her voice, hug her and "absorb" her!

But, there were other important people there for that special day. You see, the biological father was also there! I got to actually see the first time that they saw each other and it was very healing. And, his wife was there too experience this moment of GRACE!

There were lots of conversations, lots of laughs and a lot of food that were a part of that day and every bit of it was great! It seemed like a dream! The daughter's husband, best friend and cousins were there also. (And, someone actually videoed it all! YAY! - I actually have already said this, but now that you know it is ME, it means more, right?)

And, if I could only somehow add the video right here...it was a wonderful dream come true.

At the end of the day, me, Darrell, the biological father and his wife were all at one table. Let me say that again. All at one table, with the daughter being the center of attention. They all sat at a table full of answers, laughter, tears and healing.

That table was also full of adoption! The only person at the table that wasn't adopted was Darrell! It was amazing to see God's plan coming together, right there. IN HIS TIMING!

You may be a little confused when I say that everyone at the table was adopted. YES! We all were except my husband. The biological father and his wife were also adopted. That is a lot of GOD'S PLAN all at one table!

Forgiveness was given and unconditional love was shown to me. The past was washed away. (Remember that prayer that was prayed over us? It was my friend Damian that texted me that prayer just a few minutes before I met my biological daughter.)

I need to add something that is important to me. My husband Darrell knew about me having a baby before we started dating. I remember him telling me that he needed to talk to me and so I went to his house. He sat down and began telling me that he knew my past. I quickly got up and grabbed my car keys. I was leaving. I wasn't leaving because I was upset he found out, I was leaving because I thought he was breaking up with me. My past was filled with my shame. I was totally wrong because all Darrell said was that he wanted to date me even more than he did before because he admired what I did. WHAT? No wonder I married him. I thought my heart would burst when he told me that because I thought I was "damaged goods." A lie I told myself.

Another lie that I told myself was that everyone thought bad of me. I talked a little bit about going to a small school. Well, everyone at that school found out about me. I think even the janitor knew! And since it happened my senior year, I felt like I was the "talk of the town" all summer long after graduation. I am sure that there were those that said negative things, and you know, if they did, they did. Right now, I feel like I need to mention my friend Patrick again. He was a year behind me at school, so he heard a lot of talk. He defended me through all of it! And he never has made me feel anything but positive things about myself, still to this day! I literally thought that he was one of the few that didn't think horrible things about me. Another lie. Even though I was feeling alone, and talked about, I learned that the many friends and teachers and parents of friends that I had before graduation, still loved me the same after I had the baby. I remember when I finally got up the nerve to go back to church, I felt like a spotlight was on me. But looking back, it was GOD'S LIGHT shining on me. I was showing people that you can make it through hard times, and in my own way, I was an example of strength. I sure didn't feel very strong, but God gave me the strength I needed.

And one more lie that I told myself is that God would punish me for what I had done. I thought that when I had my miscarriage. I convinced myself that I was to blame when we lost the baby. It is amazing what your brain can make you believe. I should have listened to my heart because my heart knew better. Papa God does not work that way. We are and can never be "damaged goods"to God. He will never think bad of us and is not the kind of Lord that "pays back" when we struggle. He loves every single thing about me and He loves every single thing about you too.

I cannot begin to explain all of the emotions that I have felt in the past months since I got that first message. I can breathe, I can heal, I can feel forgiven. I am also forming a relationship with my biological daughter that is so "cool" (we both describe it that way!) and it seems like it is a new relationship but it has been there a long time. I know that sounds weird, but it is true. I am learning all about a new person in my life that has always been there. And, SHE is proof that God answers prayers!

I feel like this also needs to be mentioned.again. The song, New Wine. Let me tell you again that I sang that song over and over. I loved it. I had no idea that when I was crying out to God by singing the words to this song, that the Lord was already doing that in my life. Part of the song also talks about not having to understand what the Lord is doing. Wow! Little did I know what was coming in my life. Please PLEASE go back and read the lyrics.

Thankful for that song! Thankful for the freedom I feel! Thankful I don't carry around those "old flames" of doubt, low self-esteem, and being unforgiven anymore! AND...I am thankful for my biological daughter's diaper bag with that precious information hidden in it! That is how she found me!

I also need to mention another song that I sang the SAME night that I got that first message. The song is "The Blessing" and for those who have heard it, it simply states that Papa God's favor will be on your children. *Again, WOW!*

Now, I need to close because I know this is a lot. Trust me, I have lived it.

I stated that I found my purpose, right?

MY PURPOSE IS TO HELP EVERYONE KNOW THAT
EVERYTHING IS IN GOD'S TIMING!

But what I didn't realize is that God was SHOWING me that everything in MY life has been HIS PLAN AND in HIS TIMING. *And He has
had a purpose for my life.*

And I have to share my story. I feel like I would not be honoring God if
I keep this to myself. I have to TELL MY STORY TO HELP EVERYONE
SEE PROOF THAT EVERYTHING IS IN GOD'S TIMING!

(I have already shared my story with someone who is very important to
me. My friend has been going through some issues with her husband and
we were at a monthly girl's night dinner with my sister-in-law Deneen, my
cousin Rachelle, and this friend. She was telling her story and saying she was
frustrated at God for allowing trials in her husband's life, and I pulled out
the upcoming picture and just blurted out my whole entire story! I told her
that everything that was happening in their life was God's plan and God's
timing. The amount of encouragement I got from sharing and the support
I have gotten from these women is incredible!)

Now...back on track!

I am adopted. My brother is adopted. I had a baby that was adopted
by a wonderful family. I adopted my youngest child. My very best friend is
adopted. I have wonderful children, a wonderful husband and a wonderful
life. And all of this happened because God had every single moment of my
life planned out for me. Even through those hard times, He never left my side.
And at all of the high points in my life, He was there also. All of the puzzle
pieces fit together. ALL OF MY PUZZLE PIECES FIT TOGETHER!

I challenge you to do two things. First of all, FIND YOUR PURPOSE.
When you live KNOWING your purpose, it makes life so much sweeter. If
something happens in your life that takes you off track, upsets you or makes
you question things, it is easier to cope knowing your purpose! When you

are on top of that "mountain" and feel like the world is on your side, or when you are at your lowest "valley" and feel like you can't go on...Bring yourself BACK to YOUR PURPOSE!

And second, always ALWAYS know that God will never leave YOUR SIDE. He loves you so much. Let him help you fit your "life puzzle pieces" together. He can.

I AM PROOF!

*UPDATE! Before I finished writing this, I got to actually tell my biological daughter HAPPY BIRTHDAY on her ACTUAL BIRTHDAY this year AND, she has actually visited me at my "dream home!" By the way, the diaper bag in my story was HER diaper bag!

Me and My Biological Daughter

NOV 30, 2020, 3:12 PM

Hello! So this may be a weird and random question, but does September 22, 1988 mean anything to you?

DEC 07, 2020, 7:03 AM

Yes

The ACTUAL message

My life-long friend Margaret

Me and my husband Darrell. I would not have been able to make it through all of this without his support. Thank you Darrell. More!

Ecclesiastes 3:1–8

A Time for Everything

1 For everything there is a season, and a time for every matter under heaven:
2 a time to be born, and a time to die;
a time to plant, and a time to pluck up what is planted;
3 a time to kill, and a time to heal;
a time to break down, and a time to build up;
4 a time to weep, and a time to laugh;
a time to mourn, and a time to dance;
5 a time to cast away stones, and a time to gather
stones together;
a time to embrace, and a time to refrain from embracing;
6 a time to seek, and a time to lose;
a time to keep, and a time to cast away;
7 a time to tear, and a time to sew;
a time to keep silence, and a time to speak;
8 a time to love, and a time to hate;
a time for war, and a time for peace.

THE END...or another beginning?

CPSIA information can be obtained
at www.ICGtesting.com
Printed in the USA
LVHW011653030322
712534LV00008B/184

9 781662 841439